WHO LIVES HERE?

DEEP SEA

Mary-Jane Wilkins

BROWN BEAR BOOKS

Published by Brown Bear Books Ltd

4877 N. Circulo Bujia
Tucson, AZ 85718
USA

and

First Floor
9–17 St Albans Place
London N1 0NX

© 2017 Brown Bear Books Ltd

ISBN 978-1-78121-345-2

Library of Congress Cataloging-in-Publication Data available on request

Picture Researcher: Clare Newman
Desiner: Melissa Roskell
Design Manager: Keith Davis
Editorial Director: Lindsey Lowe
Children's Publisher: Anne O'Daly

Printed in China

Picture Credits

The photographs in this book are used by permission and through the courtesy of:

Front Cover: NOAA: cl; Shutterstock: tl, Willyam Bradberry main, Ethan Daniels bl, Richard Whitcombe br;
Inside: 1, ©Shutterstock/Super Joseph; 4, ©NOAA; 4-5, ©Shutterstock/Willyam Bradberry; 6, ©FLPA/Norbert Wu/Minden Pictures; 6-7, ©Shutterstock/Super Joseph; 8, ©Getty Images/Bill Curtsinger/National Geographic; 8-9, ©Photoshot/Paula de Oliveira/NHPA; 10, ©Nature PL/David Shale; 10-11, ©Nature PL/David Shale; 12, ©Nature PL/David Shale; 13, ©Shutterstock/Ethan Daniels; 14, ©Shutterstock/Eric Isselee; 14-15, ©FLPA/Reinhard Dirscherl; 16, ©Corbis/National Geographic Creative; 16-17, ©FLPA/Norbert Wu/Minden Pictures; 18, ©Corbis/Thomas P. Peschak/National Geographic; 18-19, ©Shutterstock/Andreas Fenkie; 20, ©NOAA; 21, ©FLPA/Photo Researchers; 22, ©Shutterstock/Super Joseph; 23, ©Shutterstock/Stefan Pircher.
T=Top, C=Center, B=Bottom, L=Left, R=Right

Brown Bear Books has made every attempt to contact the copyright holder. If you have any information please contact:
licensing@brownbearbooks.co.uk

CONTENTS

Where Is the DEEPEST SEA?

Near land, the sea is shallow. About 40 miles (65 km) from shore, the ocean gets deeper. The deepest parts are trenches. The deepest trench is in the Pacific Ocean.

Some animals in the deep, dark sea make their own light.

WOW!

Sea covers nearly
three-quarters of the Earth.
There are five oceans.
The Pacific Ocean is
the **biggest**.

Arctic
Ocean

Atlantic
Ocean

Pacific
Ocean

Indian
Ocean

Southern
Ocean

The deeper you go in the ocean,
the darker it gets. It is completely
dark below 3,280 feet (1,000 m).
You can read about some
deep-sea animals in this book.

ANGLERFISH

Anglerfish live in the deep sea. A female anglerfish has a **huge** head. A spine pokes out of the top of it. The end of the spine lights up.

Prey see the light at the end of the spine and swim toward it.

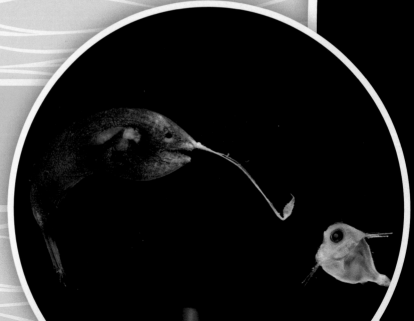

Anglerfish can eat eels and squid that are twice as **big** as themselves.

DEEP-SEA SHARKS

Lots of sharks live in the deep sea.
The cookie-cutter shark is not very big.
It can grow to 20 inches (50 cm) long,
but it has very sharp front teeth.

WOW!
Cookie-cutter
sharks can give
bigger animals
a nasty bite.

The goblin shark eats mollusks, fish, and crabs. When the shark senses food nearby, its jaws shoot forward. They snap around the prey and suck it into the shark's mouth.

DEEP-SEA SQUID

Many squid live in the deep sea, 1,000 feet (305 m) below the surface. The **biggest** squid is the colossal squid. It can be longer than a bus!

WOW!

Deep-sea squid have **big** eyes. They help the squid find food in the deep, dark ocean.

Squid **grab** their prey with their **long** armlike tentacles. They eat fish, crabs, and shrimp.

GLASS SPONGE

These animals live at the bottom of the sea.
They are called glass sponges because their
spikes are made of the same material as glass.
They fix onto rocks on the seabed and each other.

Glass sponges eat tiny
creatures that float
in the water
around them.

A sea cucumber does not have a shell or bones. Its body is full of liquid. This helps the animal move around.

SEA CUCUMBER

The sea cucumber feeds on tiny plants and animals, and scraps from the seabed. It can bury itself in the sandy sea floor.

SPERM WHALE

These **huge** whales can grow to 59 feet (18 m) long. They can dive down 3,280 feet (1,000 m) to look for food. A sperm whale can eat 1.5 tons (1.36 tonnes) of food in a day!

Whales breathe through a blowhole in their head.

Sperm whales have the **biggest** brain of any animal. They live in groups called pods.

GULPER EEL

These long, black eels live deep down in cold, dark water. A gulper eel has a **huge** mouth that opens very wide. It can eat animals as big as itself!

The gulper eel eats fish that swim toward the light on the end of the eel's tail.

This eel has a very **l o n g** tail that helps it move through the water.

CUTTLEFISH

A cuttlefish has eight arms and two tentacles. There are suckers on all of them. The tentacles **grab** prey and pull it toward the cuttlefish's mouth.

WOW!

If a cuttlefish spots a predator, it can let out a cloud of **black ink** and hide in it.

Cuttlefish can change color to blend in with the background. This helps them catch fish, crabs, and shrimp.

TRIPOD FISH

A tripod fish is just 14 inches (36 cm) long. But its three stiff fins can be 3 feet (1 m) long. The fish sits on the fins at the bottom of the sea. It waits for prey.

WOW!

This fish is also called a stilt walker because of the way it moves.

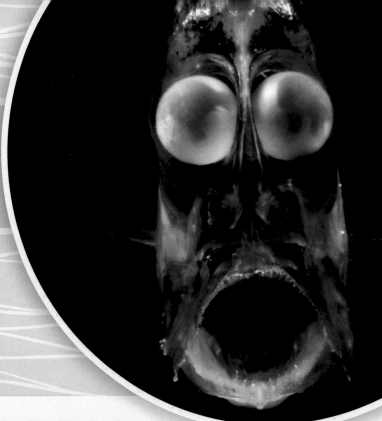

Hatchetfish have **big**, glowing eyes. They help the fish see food that falls from above.

HATCHETFISH

This fish is named for the shape of its body. It is very thin and looks like the blade of a hatchet. Hatchetfish make their own light in the deep, dark sea.

DEEP SEA FACTS

 The deepest seabed is called Challenger Deep. It is in the Pacific Ocean. It is nearly 7 miles (11 km) deep.

 The longest mountain range in the world is underwater. It is called the Mid-Oceanic Ridge. It is more than 35,000 miles (56,000 km) long.

 Most deep sea fish have very big eyes. The eyes help them use every bit of light.

USEFUL WORDS

mollusk

An animal with a soft body.
Most mollusks have a hard shell.
A snail is a mollusk.

predator

An animal that hunts and
kills other animals for food.
Cuttlefish are predators. →

prey

An animal hunted and eaten by another
animal. Fish are the prey of cuttlefish.

trench

A deep underwater ditch.

FIND OUT MORE

Deep Sea Creatures—Kids Explore series CreateSpace Independent Publishing Platform, 2014

Little Kids First Big Book of the Ocean Catherine D Hughes, National Geographic, 2013

The Usborne Book of Big Sea Creatures Minna Lacey, Usborne, 2011

Weird Sea Creatures Laura Marsh, National Geographic Society Readers, 2012

INDEX